ACTORS ON SHAKESPEARE

Twelfth Night; or, What You Will EMMA FIELDING

Emma Fielding was born in Catterick, North Yorkshire. She studied acting at the Royal Scottish Academy of Music and Drama. In 1993 she played in *School for Wives* at the Almeida Theatre, London (for which she received the Ian Charleson Award) and in Tom Stoppard's *Arcadia* at the Royal National Theatre, London (for which she received the London Critics' Circle Most Promising Newcomer award). For the Royal Shakespeare Company she has played Viola in *Twelfth Night* (for which she won the Peggy Ashcroft Award for Best Actress), Hermia in *A Midsummer Night's Dream* and Penthea in *The Broken Heart*. Her most recent work has been at the Royal Court in 2001 in Rebecca Gilman's *Spinning into Butter*, and in the West End (2001) and on Broadway (2002) in Noel Coward's *Private Lives*. She has made numerous television, film and radio appearances. She lives in London.

Colin Nicholson is the originator and editor for the Actors on Shakespeare series published by Faber and Faber.

EMMA FIELDING

Twelfth Night; or, What You Will

Series Editor: Colin Nicholson

faber and faber

First published in 2002
by Faber and Faber Limited
3 Queen Square London WC1N 3AU

Typeset by Faber and Faber in Minion
Printed in England by Mackays of Chatham plc

A CIP record for this book is available from the British Library

ISBN 0–571–21402–9

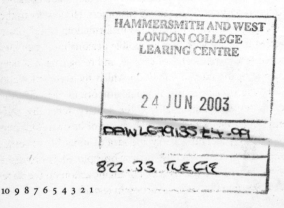

10 9 8 7 6 5 4 3 2 1

Introduction

Shakespeare: Playwright, Actor and Actors' Playwright

It is important to remember that William Shakespeare was an actor, and his understanding of the demands and rewards of acting helped him as a playwright to create roles of such richness and depth that actors in succeeding generations – even those with no reason or desire to call themselves 'classical' actors – have sought opportunities to perform them.

As the company dramatist, Shakespeare was writing under the pressure of producing scripts for almost immediate performance by his fellow players – the Lord Chamberlain's Men (later the King's Men), who, as a share-holding group, had a vested interest in their playhouse. Shakespeare was writing for a familiar set of actors: creating roles for particular players to interpret; and, being involved in a commercial enterprise, he was sensitive to the direct contact between player and audience and its power to bring in paying customers. His answer to the challenge produced a theatrical transformation: Shakespeare peopled the stage with highly credible personalities, men and women who were capable of change, and recognizable as participants in the human condition which their audience also shared. He connected two new and important elements: the idea of genuine individuality – the solitary, reflecting, self-communing soul, which is acutely aware of its own sufferings and desires; and, correlatively, the idea of inner life as something that not only exists but can also be explored. For him, the connection became the motor of dramatic action on the stage, as it is the motor of personal action in real life.

The primary importance of the actor cannot be disputed: it is his or her obligation – assisted to a greater or lesser extent by a director's overall vision of the play – to understand the personality they are representing onstage, and the nature of the frictions taking place when that personality interacts with other characters in the drama. Shakespeare's achievement goes far beyond the creation of memorable characters (Macbeth, Falstaff) to embrace the exposition of great relationships (Macbeth–Lady Macbeth; Falstaff–Prince Hal). Great roles require great actors, and there is no group of people in a better position to interpret those roles to *us* than the principal actors of *our* generation – inhabitants of a bloodline whose vigour resonates from the sixteenth century to the present day – who have immersed themselves in the details of Shakespeare's creations and have been party to their development through rehearsal and performance.

Watching Shakespeare can be an intimidating experience, especially for those who are not well versed in the text, or in the conventions of the Elizabethan stage. Many excellent books have been written for the academic market but our aim in this series is somewhat different. *Actors on Shakespeare* asks contemporary performers to choose a play of particular interest to them, push back any formal boundaries that may obstruct channels of free communication and give the modern audience a fresh, personal view. Naturally the focus for each performer is different – and these diverse volumes are anything but uniform in their approach to the task – but their common intention is, primarily, to look again at plays that some audiences may know well and others not at all, as well as providing an insight into the making of a performance.

Each volume works in its own right, without assuming an in-depth knowledge of the play, and uses substantial quotation to contextualize the principal points. The fresh approach of the many and varied writers will, we hope, enhance your enjoyment of Shakespeare's work.

Colin Nicholson
February 2002

Note: For reference, the text used here is the Arden Shakespeare.

Characters

Duke Orsino *of Illyria*
Countess Olivia
Malvolio, *her steward*
Sir Toby Belch, *her uncle*
Sir Andrew Aguecheek, *her suitor*
Feste, *her jester*
Maria, *her chambermaid*
Fabian, *an upper servant*
Viola
Sebastian, *her twin brother*
Antonio, *a sea captain, his friend*
Attendants, Captain, Lords (*including* Curio *and* Valentine),
   Musicians, Officers, Priest, Sailors

Twelfth Night; or, What You Will was performed by the Royal Shakespeare Company at Stratford-upon-Avon in May 1994, with the following cast:

Viola	Emma Fielding
Orsino	Clive Wood
Curio	Gwynn Beech
Valentine	Glenn Hugill
Olivia	Haydn Gwynne
Sir Toby Belch	Tony Britton
Maria	Joanna McCallum
Sir Andrew Aguecheek	Billie Brown
Feste	Derek Griffiths
Malvolio	Desmond Barrit
Fabian	Robert Gillespie
Sebastian	Robert Bowman
Antonio	Steven Elliott
Sea Captain/Priest	James Barriscale

Directed by Ian Judge

Foreword

My experience of *Twelfth Night* came through playing Viola off and on for eighteen months with the Royal Shakespeare Company; and like the man playing the doctor in *A Streetcar Named Desire* who, when asked what the play was about, allegedly replied, 'It's about this doctor . . .', so inevitably, when asked about *Twelfth Night*, I'd say, 'It's about this ship-wrecked girl . . .' She was my way into the play, into Illyria – a peculiar place: in reality a province in the Balkans in what is now Croatia, but in the world of the play a place where people are infected by the madness of love and the dead come back to life. Comedy springs from an accumulation of concealment – of identities and feelings – causing such confusion that the truth has to burst out and order is eventually restored. And the whole is tempered with a particularly English melancholy that comes from sunny autumns and damp summers – 'for the rain it raineth every day'.

Viola was my first professional experience of Shakespeare and it was an extremely joyful one. I learned priceless fundamental lessons that can only be truly absorbed by working on the part professionally and in the context of a season at the Royal Shakespeare Company. I drank in all the advice I was given by the hugely experienced people that I was surrounded by; I watched and listened. I rapidly realized that nothing prepares you for professional work like professional work – a terrible catch-22 situation for actors trying to start their working lives who, through no want of talent and determination, have to wait for their first engagements. Extraordinarily simple things became apparent very quickly – for example,

1

the fact that turning up on time with your homework done (be it lines learnt or research into the play, prompted or unprompted by the director, completed) is vital and certainly requires no artistic talent. I'd spent the first couple of years of my career apologizing for being an actor. I lied about my profession frequently. Playing Viola in addition to Hermia in *A Midsummer Night's Dream* and Penthea in John Ford's *The Broken Heart*, in repertoire, often rehearsing one play during the day and performing another in the evening, made me stop apologizing and 'come out' as an actor. I realized I was serving a never-ending apprenticeship, vital to any profession. When the learning stops, the acting does too. At its best, acting is an interpretive skill up there with those of the concert violinist and the opera singer – and no one ever asks Pavarotti when he's going to get a proper job, or if he enjoys being part of the second oldest profession.

I learned how to fill the gaping void of the Royal Shakespeare Theatre in Stratford-upon-Avon both vocally and physically. I also learned not to be afraid of pure theatricality. My approach had always been a rigidly psychologically-based one: I always needed a reason for every move and action. I was asked one day in rehearsals to make a bold, sweeping move across the stage, which I was more than willing to do, but I felt I needed a reason. I was told simply to show off the back of my coat. I balked initially, but then it became a release for me. I would find a psychological reason, quietly, outside the rehearsal room; but in the meantime I learned simply to enjoy being on the stage, to inhabit the space completely, not to apologize. I was in a large theatre, not in a small studio space, in a radio studio or on a film set. I learned to relish being there. I began to keep my head up so that the people in the cheap seats could see my eyes and therefore what I was thinking. And I learned to be audible. What is the point of creating the most intricately truthful portrayal of a character if the audience can't see or hear you? I came to see that psychological truth and theatricality weren't mutually exclusive, but could coexist and enhance each other.

The Lovers

Finding Viola

Viola and her ability to adapt to every situation helped me to realize that, as an actor, you adapt to the situation that you find yourself in. You adapt to the director, and not the other way round. I worked with three very different directors in three very different roles, and the route to professional and personal happiness was to listen and embrace wholeheartedly the working environment they were each trying to create. Above all I learned that, no matter how rigid or free the atmosphere, the final performance depends on the uniquely individual actors brought together for that particular project. In the most rigidly blocked production, the character is still yours, created by you and the other actors on the stage; and as I came to Viola first out of the three, I credit her with helping me to make that discovery. She also introduced me to Shakespeare in a living, breathing incarnation; his words were made flesh. She allowed me to speak his words aloud in a large auditorium, to use his language as was intended by the playwright, as a means of communicating with an audience, not simply as a subject for academic dissertation. She guided me through the play; I simply followed the clues that were waiting for me in the endlessly robust text that took any amount of re-examination and deconstruction in the course of an eighteen-month run. It was exhilarating and uplifting to perform every time, even when at the start of the play it was occasionally very hard to shake off the outside world.

I remember one matinee towards the end of the run of *Twelfth Night*. I had torn ligaments, a hangover and two performances of Viola ahead of me. I felt exhausted. Someone from the wig department threw a bucket of water over me to simulate the effects of the shipwreck, and then I stumbled over the waiting stage crew in the dark to take up my position. Sitting in the dark. Still. Waiting. I felt guilty and sick. Expectant audience, expensive seats, and I was about to ruin it for them. Because I didn't feel like doing the play. I was fed up, weepy, and feeble surges of adrenalin were trying to kick in, so that flight not fight seemed the only option. It was a shock to feel apathy. No one told me there'd be days like this.

A rebirth, I suppose

The production had Viola emerging from billowing silk waves on to an empty shore, accompanied solely by the Captain of the wrecked ship – a rebirth, I suppose, and also the only time in the play when she is openly female and openly vulnerable. I sat shivering in the dark behind the backcloth that was Orsino's chamber. The Captain, dressed only in leather trousers and a long wig reminiscent of a seventies heavy-rock fan, picked me up in his arms. I really felt sick now. Nowhere to run. *What the hell am I doing here?* The storm music started up. He moved forward through the yards of flowing material into the light – into Illyria.

Suddenly there was no time to be curmudgeonly, self-indulgent. I had to be active, alive, living in the moment – like Viola. The banality of the outside world – the snarling London traffic, the ludicrous life that I was living, the half-eaten sandwich curling in my dressing room and, most of all, the fear of disappointing 900 theatregoers – vanished instantly. I never thought I'd be grateful to a fictional character, unless under the influence of heavy medication, but that's what happened that afternoon. It was her – Viola. I had lived with her for eighteen months and she carried me, she supported me, improvising a new way of existing for herself, with her exuberant lust for life. She saved me. I suppose I fell for her.

Initially I find myself looking for parallels with my own life, whoever I'm playing. The play sits on the page before me, an edifice of words, and I'm standing outside it, trying to find a way in – not so that I can simply say, 'Hey the character's just like *me*,' but in order to find a touchstone, an emotional way in, a kick start for the imagination. If it doesn't ring true for the actor, how can an audience be expected to believe it? You become a magpie. You're constantly searching for information, consciously or unconsciously. Suddenly the newspapers, radio or television will appear to have relevant snippets of experience; a piece of music may help you in, an anecdote. The world becomes a place of coincidences, synchronicity, as you endeavour to tap in to a collective consciousness.

My mother is a twin

More often than not a part finds you when you're ready. A personal experience gives you an understanding unavailable before. You're open to it. Viola is a twin. My mother is an identical twin. Her twin sister died not long before I started rehearsing the play. Another friend who had lost a sister said, 'That's my dream,' when told I was to start rehearsing the play. I didn't know what they meant. 'My dream . . . I dream my sister's not dead and I turn a corner and suddenly she's there.' The dream of the bereaved, the dead come back to life, and twins are twins for ever. OK, so some would accuse me of emotional cannibalism – for what? Just a play? But there is such a strong responsibility to the audience, and not just because they've paid. Some of them will have been bereaved, will have fallen in love, felt suicidal – whatever. It's my job to portray that as truthfully as is humanly possible, to tap into the collective consciousness, so as not to insult the people sitting in the dark; and to try to make it something more than just a play – perhaps something cathartic, comforting, uplifting and also entertaining.

The first question I ever asked about Viola was: 'Why doesn't she just go home?' She has some gold, part or all of which she gives to the Captain when he gives her a glimmer of hope about Sebastian's survival: 'For saying so, there's gold.'

She's a young, unchaperoned noblewoman, shipwrecked abroad, and her first inquiry about the land of her shipwreck is: 'Who governs here?' – effectively: 'Who's in charge here?' (This was, to me, reminiscent of the cry of the stranded English upper classes abroad.) If she is of noble birth, the chances are she is acquainted with them, or even related, as is the case with the British Royal Family and most of the crowned and usurped heads of Europe. The Sea Captain informs her that the Duke Orsino rules Illyria. What about her remaining family? Home is not too remote, as Orsino has been mentioned by her father – 'Orsino! I have heard my father name him' – and Sebastian even names it as Messaline – 'my father was that Sebastian of Messaline whom I know you have heard of' – believed to be derived from the Latin for Marseilles, not an insuperable distance from Illyria, if we're literal about it. And why was she on the ship with only Sebastian and no other mentioned relatives or friends in the first place? Where were they going? Why? These questions may seem too literal and obvious, but in order to understand where Viola and Sebastian derive their energy, openness and gift for survival from, they needed answering before I leapt into the narrative of the play itself.

The twins' father is the only parent mentioned in the text in a warm, anecdotal way – 'My father had a daughter lov'd a man', 'My father had a mole upon his brow', and, as mentioned above, 'Orsino! I have heard my father name him.' Sebastian does mention their mother, but only in reference to his being near to tears: '. . . and I am yet so near the manners of my mother, that upon the least occasion more mine eyes will tell tales of me', which feels more like a figure of speech than an evocation of a lachrymose parent. So this was all the family background the actor playing Sebastian and I had to go on. We decided to imagine a plausible prequel. The details were sketchy at first, but we needed an imaginative tool to get inside the heads of these boisterous, marvellous twins. Why would a young noblewoman, for example, dress up as a page and decide to serve a stranger rather than seek his help as a fellow member of the nobility? And why would her twin decide to marry a noblewoman he has just met, even though he suspects that both she and he may be completely barking?

We decided that our mother had died in childbirth, as the delivery of twins can be complicated (even today, with advanced medicine and technology) and they had arrived as they meant to go on, kicking and screaming. They were doted on and brought up by a widower father. He subsequently died when they were thirteen, as mentioned in the final scene, and they were bereft. They inherited when they reached their majority; there was nothing left for them at home, so they sold everything, boarded a ship and went off to explore the world: new horizons, escape from the loss of their beloved father – displacement as the ultimate displacement activity, so to speak.

So when Viola is washed up, freezing, soaking and exhausted, believing her brother – her *twin* brother, her only remaining relative – to be drowned, her possessions lost at sea save for the clothes she stands up in and a purse that she clung to as the ship went down, what is she to do? How is she to live, to continue, emotionally and practically? With the simple story that we devised, just for us (I don't think we told the director, and I don't know how much of it showed in our performances), the stakes were as high as they could have been for both of us. I think that, until the Captain tells her that there is a slim chance Sebastian may have survived, she is ready to throw herself back into the sea; but as long as there is some hope, she is willing to exist. Her resilience and practicality immediately come into play and, in order to continue living, she finds what she thinks is a way of becoming invisible. Her old world is destroyed and, to prevent herself from dwelling on the death of her brother, she tries to create a safe haven for herself where she can recover. The aftermath of the wreck is a relatively short scene, but in terms of determining the rest of the play and showing her remarkable resilience it is crucial. Her actions unwittingly trigger off the whole chain of events that leads to an inexorable spiral of chaos. When she hears of Olivia's situation (the double bereavement of father and brother), she is immediately drawn to her and sees an opportunity to hide in a sympathetic environment as a servant (someone invisible), until she is ready to face the world as herself:

> O that I serv'd that lady,
> And might not be deliver'd to the world,
> Till I had made mine own occasion mellow,
> What my estate is.
>
> (Act I, scene ii)

Olivia, unfortunately, is admitting nobody to her household, such is the extent of her grief. Orsino is already familiar to Viola via her father – pure conjecture, but perhaps he was mentioning him as a possible suitor for Viola: 'He was a bachelor then.' She decides to serve him, a tenuous link with her past life, but to serve him as 'an eunuch'.

When first performed, Viola was female for as short a time as possible and her almost immediate transformation into Cesario was largely for practical reasons, as before the Restoration women's roles were played by boys; but Shakespeare also gives her a very specific reason for her action: her supposedly dead brother. She doesn't endanger herself with time for reflection and grief, for fear that it will engulf her. She throws herself into her new life as Cesario and is so skilled at it that within three days she has become Orsino's favourite and confidant. And, aside from her charm and skill, he is strangely drawn to this young boy, as she is to him. He becomes her world. But it isn't until she first hears the mention of Sebastian's name that she finally tells the audience (who, apart from the Captain and perhaps Feste, are the only ones to know her true identity) her devastating motives for dressing as she does:

> He nam'd Sebastian. I my brother know
> Yet living in my glass; even such and so
> In favour was my brother, and he went
> Still in this fashion, colour, ornament,
> For him I imitate.
>
> (Act III, scene iv)

She has become her dead twin. She is no longer Viola, and every time she looks in the mirror, Sebastian is alive. She is also, presumably, safer as a man in a strange environment – and consider the physical as well as social freedom she can enjoy compared to what would be allowed her as a female.

Conceived in the moment

So why doesn't she go home? Well there's nothing for her to go back to. These are the high stakes – much more exhilarating to play and more dramatic to watch than a pale-faced waif wafting round passively. Of course Viola is reactive (a quality ascribed to her in a pejorative sense by some literary critics), but that's borne out of emotional and practical necessity rather than an inability to be proactive. She wholeheartedly embraces the truism 'Time is a great healer.' Her plan for existence is impulsive, conceived in the moment, but she throws herself into it, trusting to the only certainty for her in the chaotic newness of her untried existence: Time. Day will become night and night turn to day again – that is the only guarantee she has as she leaves to become Cesario. Time becomes a tangible, comforting force for her. She clings to it as to an old friend: 'What else may hap, to time I will commit.'

Orsino

Now what about Orsino, the man she has made her shot in the dark? I just think he's not very good with girls. He is a soldier in a household full of men (Antonio's only knowledge of him is as such:

> I do not without danger walk these streets.
> Once in a sea-fight 'gainst the Count his galleys,
> I did some service,
>> (Act III , scene iii)

and he fears for his life), and he's laying siege to Olivia determined not to be defeated. I always assumed he was a soldier, a hot-headed, battle-scarred veteran, even though throughout the play he is a man possessed by love. Perhaps that was some rather dodgy wishful thinking on my part, making him border on the wrong side of a rugged yet appealingly flawed Mills and Boon alpha male (the old archetypes are the best), but it was the nature of his passion that convinced me of it, and also his dialogue with Antonio, which states that they fought against each other in a sea battle or, at the very least, Orsino was close enough to have a very good view:

> That face of his I do remember well;
> Yet when I saw it last, it was besmear'd
> As black as Vulcan, in the smoke of war.
> A baubling vessel was he captain of,
> For shallow draught and bulk unprizable,
> With which such scathful grapple did he make
> With the most noble bottom of our fleet,
> That very envy and the tongue of loss
> Cried fame and honour on him.
> (Act V, scene i)

His passion has a dogged, determined quality. He never stops to consider the possibility of eventual defeat, he wants victory at all costs. He is lovesick, full to the brim with unrequited passion. He feels hounded by love:

> That instant was I turn'd into a hart,
> And my desires, like fell and cruel hounds,
> E'er since pursue me.
> (Act I, scene i)

He certainly doesn't appear, through his language, to be an aesthete lying around on some nice cushions. Viola is passionate and impulsive, and in Orsino she has unwittingly met her match.

After just three days she is not only a favoured servant but also (and this cannot be explained away by the simple fact that a new face around the house is a novelty) a valued confidant: 'I have unclasp'd / To thee the book even of my secret soul.' As I said earlier, he is 'strangely drawn' to this curiously feminine boy.

What can, to some, seem arrogance in the face of constant rebuttal from Olivia I always saw as a rather admirable constancy, although of course infuriating for the recipient of endless unsolicited advances. He is so blinkered in his aims that, rather than sympathizing with Olivia's desire to mourn her double loss for seven years in isolation, he sees it as a measure of her capacity to love and becomes overwhelmed with the fantasy of her directing all her mourning towards him as some sort of emotional tidal wave:

> O, she that hath a heart of that fine frame
> To pay this debt of love but to a brother,
> How will she love, when the rich golden shaft
> Hath kill'd the flock of all affections else
> That live in her; when liver, brain, and heart,
> These sovereign thrones, are all supplied, and fill'd
> Her sweet perfections with one self king!
>   (Act I, scene i)

Poor sod, he just doesn't get it. And there is something rather touching in his emotional immaturity. But just as he is constant and consistent, so he demands loyalty and constancy from those around him. He is the Duke of Illyria, with absolute authority and the lonely burden of being a ruler – which is precisely why he has become so blinkered. He has no confidant, no one to reflect with or, I suppose, to show his feminine side to. I imagine he's not good at small talk. Even he says, 'I myself am best / When least in company.' Eat your heart out, Greta Garbo.

Then along comes Viola, an outsider, recently bereaved, so she believes. And he can speak to her. She's vulnerable, trying to be unobtrusive and invisible, and, of course, becomes the most curious, fascinating addition to the household. She is drawn into the confidence of this flawed, lonely, passionate older man at the lowest point of her existence so far, and of course she falls for him. It would be peculiar if she didn't.

Confusion

Viola is sent on her first mission to Olivia's household: 'Be clamorous, and leap all civil bounds, / Rather than make unprofited return.' She has to gain entry at all costs. Orsino sees her as his secret weapon, where his staff have previously failed, this young, feminine boy is bound to succeed. She enters into the bargain and will strive her utmost for the man she has now fallen for hook, line and sinker. And the words burst out of her in her first address to the audience: 'yet, a barful strife! / Whoe'er I woo, myself would be his wife.' Such a relief to be herself and to unburden her heart. The complicity with the audience, after initially being the most terrifying part of the performance – you're so exposed as an actor and character – became the most relaxing part to play. She is entirely herself, Viola not Cesario, and can talk to the audience who know her more thoroughly than does anyone in the play, except Sebastian. They let some steam out of the pressure cooker for her. If she didn't have this relief, she'd be an entirely different girl.

That first contact with the audience shows Viola's clear-eyed acknowledgement of the ludicrous position in which she now finds herself. If she only knew that she is still near the beginning of a five-act play and in a short space of time Olivia, after just one meeting, will be in love with her and the circle will be complete. Orsino loves Olivia, who loves Viola, who loves Orsino. For order and harmony to be restored, a fourth person needs to appear and someone in the circle has to turn round and notice what has been under their noses all the time. Viola has been infected with the madness of love and realizes it immediately. Although she is in disguise there are glimpses of her true self and passions throughout the play, even to the point where she comes close to revealing her true identity to Orsino. Imagine having to win the heart of your rival on behalf of the person you love. That is Viola's task.

Why does Olivia let Viola in? She has vowed to be cloistered for seven years. Mind you, as in *Love's Labour's Lost*, whenever a vow like that is made in a Shakespearean comedy, it's usually a case of when will it be broken rather than will it be broken at all. How does Viola succeed where others have failed? Her dogged persistence for one thing; but it seems to be Malvolio's description of her that excites Olivia's curiosity:

OLIVIA Tell him, he shall not speak with me.

MALVOLIO 'Has been told so: and he says he'll stand at your door like a sheriff's post, and be the supporter to a bench, but he'll speak with you.

OLIVIA What kind o' man is he?

MALVOLIO Why, of mankind.

OLIVIA What manner of man?

MALVOLIO Of very ill manner: he'll speak with you, will you or no.

OLIVIA Of what personage and years is he?

MALVOLIO Not yet old enough for a man, nor young enough for a boy: as a squash is before 'tis a peascod, or a codling when 'tis almost an apple. 'Tis with him in standing water, between boy and man. He is very well-favoured, and he speaks very shrewishly. One would think his mother's milk were scarce out of him.

OLIVIA Let him approach.

(Act I, scene v)

And perhaps Malvolio's infuriating pedantry also adds to her spur-of-the-moment decision to see Viola.

Viola finally bursts into Olivia's house with great energy and not a little irritation. She has followed her instructions to the letter, serving the man she loves – with also the shadowy precursor of their final relationship:

ORSINO
  Prosper well in this,
And thou shalt live as freely as thy lord,
To call his fortunes thine.
 (Act I, scene iv)

She has her speech ready, wants to get on with it and leave. Above all she is not personally well disposed towards Olivia, to say the least. Any hope of beautiful, studied wooing disappears immediately. She has suffered a barrage of pomposity from Malvolio and incoherence from Sir Toby at the gates. She is on her guard and wary of being tricked. She doesn't suffer fools gladly, has the measure of Malvolio immediately and tars the whole household with the same brush. But there is a relish and vigour in her speech even in adversity. She is alive to every nuance, fights back at every turn, and her bravado and cheek cut through convention. She is rude. What a relief for Olivia, a distraction from her mourning and Sir Toby's tiresome behaviour. Until Viola appears it is only Feste, the other outsider, who can distract her. And he risks all by joking about the one thing closest to her heart – her brother's death:

CLOWN Good madonna, why mourn'st thou?
OLIVIA Good fool, for my brother's death.
CLOWN I think his soul is in hell, madonna.
OLIVIA I know his soul is in heaven, fool.

CLOWN The more fool, madonna, to mourn for your brother's soul, being in heaven. Take away the fool, gentlemen.

(Act I, scene v)

Viola is full of life in a house of mourning, to put it bluntly,
she's pissed off. And it is the juxtaposition of her external
identity – that of a young male servant – with what she truly is
– a well-educated female member of the nobility – that makes
her extraordinary to Olivia. Viola/Cesario has no fear, knows
the courtly rules of engagement implicitly and engages immediately with Olivia on her level in a battle of words.

All Viola wants professionally is to deliver her message to
the right person but her personal frustration bursts out:
'Most certain, if you are she, you do usurp yourself: for what
is yours to bestow is not yours to reserve. But this is from my
commission.' She chides Olivia for not loving Orsino –
something that, given her own passionate feelings, she cannot understand. And of course, although Olivia through
bereavement is mistress of her household, she is not neces-
sarily mistress of her heart. Throughout the scene her personal passion for Orsino fights with her desire to complete
her task to the best of her ability. She wants him to be happy,
for his painful passion for Olivia to be assuaged. He loves
'With adorations, fertile tears, / With groans that thunder
love, with sighs of fire . . .' This pains her, but if she is successful, she loses him to her rival. She is selfless – mostly. Or
perhaps masochistic.

I loved playing this scene: the staccato prose beginning,
when Viola wants clarity; then it grows as the speech turns to
the poetry of blank verse, the only form that can really cope
with Viola's heart-bursting passion. It turns from prose and
the prosaic – Are you really the lady of the house? – to the
soaring poetry of the 'willow cabin' speech.

Olivia is playful. Viola wants her to be serious, Orsino's love is not to be laughed at or dismissed. It's easy to forget re-reading the play that until Viola says 'let me see your face' (a bald, monosyllabic request if ever there was one) she is trying to get through to a heavily veiled woman – hence her initial scepticism that she is even addressing the lady of the house. She wants the mask to be removed. She needs to see her clearly. Then she is ambushed by Olivia's beauty. She feels inadequate, there is no comparison between them externally. Viola questions that beauty's authenticity, living in hope as always, clutching at straws. 'Excellently done, if God did all.' Human frailty – she thinks out loud unintentionally. (I came to that conclusion having tried so many different ways of playing the line; snide cattiness for the sake of a cheap laugh made no sense.) Any thought of her own attraction for Orsino evaporates in the face of Olivia's pulchritude and she already has evidence of her wit and warmth. From then on Viola's responses are heartfelt, honest and open. The masks are off. Even after Olivia has calmly and openly explained that, despite her knowledge of his many attributes, she simply doesn't love him –

> Your lord does know my mind, I cannot love him.
> Yet I suppose him virtuous, know him noble,
> Of great estate, of fresh and stainless youth;
> In voices well divulg'd, free, learn'd, and valiant,
> And in dimension and the shape of nature,
> A gracious person. But yet I cannot love him.
> He might have took his answer long ago.
>
> (Act I, scene v)

Viola persists in Orsino's cause. She cannot take no for an answer. She is subsumed completely in her own passion for him, pleading his corner with such fervour that Olivia – of

19

course – falls for her instead, just as Viola fell for Orsino as she witnessed his passion for Olivia. Who could resist the heartfelt cry that is provoked out of Viola when she has to give it her best shot? She wants Orsino to be content and, in her desperation for a positive result, unwittingly makes the situation personal to herself:

If I did love you in my master's flame,
With such a suff'ring, such a deadly life,
In your denial I would find no sense,
I would not understand it.

Olivia is now forced to examine this messenger even more closely, to see him as an individual divorced from his purely professional role. She asks, 'Why, what would you?'

VIOLA
Make me a willow cabin at your gate,
And call upon my soul within the house;
Write loyal cantons of contemned love,
And sing them loud even in the dead of night;
Halloo your name to the reverberate hills,
And make the babbling gossip of the air
Cry out 'Olivia!' O, you should not rest
Between the elements of air and earth,
But you should pity me.

All Olivia can reply to that onslaught, which seemed to hang in the air of the theatre whenever we played the scene, is: 'You might do much.'

Even after the passion of the 'willow cabin' speech, all seems lost after Olivia's simple, honest, repeated declaration: 'I cannot love him: let him send no more.' Viola hears this, but what she doesn't hear immediately is the subsequent lines: 'Unless, perchance, you come to me again, / To tell me how he takes it.' Olivia declares her hand. Viola's parting shot is a curse:

> Love make his heart of flint that you shall love,
> And let your fervour like my master's be,
> Plac'd in contempt. Farewell, fair cruelty.

a curse that ironically comes true to a degree, with Viola herself as the object of desire.

'Sex fucks up the equation'

In another time and situation I came to believe that they would instantly have forged a strong attachment anyway. Viola's generosity towards Olivia seemed to me to speak of an attraction on her part as well – a recognition. Their backgrounds, humanity, sense of mischief and of the ridiculous are similar and, although after this encounter Olivia's attraction is also overtly sexual, what a relief it would be if we could all fall in love with our best friends – not, as is often the case, have a strong, purely sexual attraction to people who are our enemies. But when you're dealing with a play that shows love and attraction in all its wild and wonderful glory, fundamental questions arise about the nature of sexuality and what attracts one human being to another.

That's the thing about love: it's either there or it's not. There's no logic, no rationale. It can't be forced, and just when everything seems to be possible, taking its logical path to a nice, tidy conclusion, along it comes to muck everything up – or, as I found scrawled in the margin of my rehearsal copy of Tom Stoppard's *Arcadia* to encapsulate just one of that play's many themes: 'Sex fucks up the equation'. In a deterministic universe, it's 'the attraction that Newton left out'.

The play is full of it. Love and attraction in so many different, wonderfully recognizable guises. Orsino, always described as being in love with love rather than with Olivia, opens the play with it. She is an idealized figure for him, distant and visual; beautiful, witty, vulnerable and bereaved – looks good in black, perhaps? But how well does he actually know her? She is high up on a pedestal and her refusal to have him makes him more determined to pursue her.

Viola sees Orsino completely – his faults and foibles – yet loves him unreservedly. She even gets infuriated with him. Her love is based on first-hand experience, domesticity. She sees him at his best and worst. And he finds her immediately indispensable. He is devoted to her although he doesn't know it. For the end of the play to work, that should be evident through all their scenes together. He doesn't know what real, long-lasting deep affection is. He thinks he wants grand opera in his life, an all-consuming passion that usurps the ability to function in any other part of it. He thinks he wants the madness, but under his nose is the person whom he truly loves and who loves him. They are best friends. As in all of Shakespeare's comedies, however, there is an element of uncertainty. The Jacks may have their Jills, but how long will the happiness last? There is resolution at the end of the play, but only for that moment. Life must continue when the curtain falls. It reminds me of the final shot of Mike Nichols' *The Graduate*. Katharine Ross and Dustin Hoffman come to rest at the back of the bus after running away from her wedding, exhilarated at what they've just done. No words are spoken. The camera holds on them unflinchingly, their smiles fade and a wonderful look of uncertainty creeps over their faces. They are together, but ultimately alone – happy momentarily, but who knows what the future will bring?

Sir Toby and Maria

Sir Toby and Maria have an understanding: 'She's a beagle, true-bred, and one that adores me: what o' that?' At the beginning of the play Sir Toby is the lesser involved of the two. He is a man past his prime, an alcoholic living off his niece. He befriends Sir Andrew – a person whom he may not even have tolerated previously – primarily perhaps for cash and sport (he can make him the butt of his jokes). He invites him on the promise of pairing him off with his niece Olivia. Sir Toby is a knight with a great future behind him, all his promise fulfilled and thrown away, or never even achieved in the first place. Curmudgeonly, quixotic, looking for sport, whether it be gulling Malvolio, bear-baiting or drinking himself into an early grave, he is searching for distractions from his own existence. Drink and sport. Maria sees all this, has no illusions about him and bides her time – full of hope, but expecting nothing. Maria instigates the initial gulling of Malvolio with her invention of the letter to be dropped in his way. But I think this has very little to do with her wanting to impress Sir Toby, even though Fabian cites this as the reason he ultimately marries her. Finally the sport begins to pall, even for Sir Toby, as the collective revenge wrought on Malvolio causes him to end up crawling around, doubting his own sanity in a darkened prison. 'I would we were well rid of this knavery' – he has gone too far and has jeopardized his very existence in Olivia's household. I always felt the simple line 'Come by and by to my chamber' is the closest he gets to expressing his feeling for her (though I am well aware that some interpret that line as being a simple instruction to Feste to report back to him later). There is a realization that he does care about something in his nihilistic existence, and that is Maria. Or perhaps he is settling for a caretaker. It's not grand opera, more comfortable slippers with no illusions whatsoever. And it is gently resolved, almost invisibly, when they marry quietly offstage. Her patience pays off and he makes an honest woman of her; or she has endangered her position with Olivia through her part in the gulling, and the least he can do is marry her. As Fabian says,

> Maria writ
> The letter, at Sir Toby's great importance,
> In recompense whereof he hath married her.
>
> (Act V, scene i)

Either way, as I've said, hardly operatic.

Sebastian

Antonio is in thrall to Sebastian. From their first appearance on stage together he cannot bear to be parted from him, continually asking where he is going and what his plans are: 'Will you stay no longer? nor will you not that I go with you?' 'Let me know of you whither you are bound.' And then, finally, 'If you will not murder me for my love, let me be your servant' – if you will not cause me to die of grief at leaving you, let me serve you. Sebastian's reply is equally heightened; he would rather die than let Antonio demean himself by waiting on him. And at the end of this short scene Antonio (a sailor who has distinguished himself in battle, no less) determines not only not to be parted from him, but literally risks his life to be with him:

> I have many enemies in Orsino's court,
> Else would I very shortly see thee there:
> But come what may, I do adore thee so,
> That danger shall seem sport, and I will go!
>
> (Act II, scene i)

He has saved Sebastian's life – '. . . you took me from the breach of the sea . . .'. To hold someone's life in your hands, to help someone cheat death, I imagine it doesn't get more intoxicating than that. In some cultures I believe it is not the *survivor* of a potentially fatal event but the *rescuer* who owes a lifelong debt to the other. They have interfered with fate, prevented someone leaving this world at their appointed time, and so the responsibility for their further existence rests with them for ever. Their lives are now inextricably linked. Perhaps there is an element of this. But there is good old-fashioned erotic attraction too (though much more on Antonio's part). The essential nature of the relationship is up for debate, but the messier and more emotionally complex the better as far as I'm concerned. There is more to be lost, it's the more satisfying option and much more poignant in the playing.

Sebastian is initially, like Viola, in shock. He has battled the waves and survived and is reeling from his sister's supposed death. Antonio is a lifeline. They subsequently spend three months together, inseparable. Antonio makes his purse freely available to him and is solicitous for his daily welfare and survival in a strange environment. Sebastian is full of gratitude and great affection for him and enjoys his company. There is a vigour and a vibrancy in his speech that suggests an exuberance and joie de vivre. He is an impetuous boy. Although mourning his sister, like her, he is full of life and possesses an openness to whatever may befall him, having already survived death once. He is, I believe, blissfully unaware of Antonio's feelings for him. He takes his generosity for granted, as not being unreasonable behaviour, because if the roles were to be reversed, he would do the same for Antonio out of simple kindness. It is not until Viola is rescued by Antonio in the duel scene that the full extent of his devotion, of his sense of personal betrayal and of his awareness of the imbalance in their relationship becomes apparent:

ANTONIO
        This youth that you see here
I snatch'd one half out of the jaws of death,
Reliev'd him with such sanctity of love;
And to his image, which methought did promise
Most venerable worth, did I devotion . . .
But O how vile an idol proves this god!
    (Act III, scene iv)

Antonio has worshipped at the shrine of Sebastian rather as Orsino has at that of Olivia; but his devotion has made him mortally vulnerable and, when rejected, he is bereft and his story is unresolved. He is left in limbo, still carrying a torch for the unattainable Sebastian.

A lost boy

I have an abiding memory of Sir Andrew Aguecheek from the Royal Shakespeare Theatre in Stratford. Our performances of *Twelfth Night* in the main house always played opposite *Coriolanus* in the Swan Theatre. Both theatres share the same backstage area. I would be backstage transforming myself into Cesario just as the Roman populace were transforming themselves into the Volscian army, covering themselves in blood, grabbing swords and generally exuding as much testosterone as is humanly possible. Through the mêlée each night, a tall, willowy figure would emerge in pink high heels and wispy blonde wig, clutching a hanky. It was Sir Andrew, weaving through the soldiers, trying not to get blood on his costume.

The contrast was of course initially amusing, but as this action was repeated night after night offstage, it seemed to emphasize Sir Andrew's existence onstage. He may be a knight but he's as incapable of raging in battle as Viola. When they are set against each other as a result of Sir Toby's and Fabian's trickery, it's hard to tell who is the more terrified, the effete knight, who may be an accomplished dancer, or the young, fragile girl, who is in danger of finally being unmasked because of her lack of physical strength.

He is a lost boy, invited by Sir Toby ostensibly to woo Olivia, but in reality '. . . he has three thousand ducats a year'. He is a source of cash. Sir Toby keeps up the front of friendship at all times, but even before Andrew's first appearance I think his real attitude towards him is pretty clear when he doesn't contradict Maria's description of him:

MARIA I heard . . . of a foolish knight that you brought in one night here to be her wooer.
SIR TOBY Who, Sir Andrew Aguecheek?
MARIA Ay, he.
SIR TOBY He's as tall a man as any's in Illyria.
MARIA What's that to th' purpose?
SIR TOBY Why, he has three thousand ducats a year.
(Act I, scene iii)

Sir Toby's so-called friendship has been purchased, unbeknown to Sir Andrew: 'I have been dear to him, lad, some two thousand strong, or so.' But it is also rapidly bankrupting him, as is shown by this exchange:

SIR TOBY Thou hadst need send for more money.
SIR ANDREW If I cannot recover your niece, I am a foul way out [of pocket].
SIR TOBY Send for money, knight; if thou hast her not i' th' end, call me cut.
(Act II, scene iii)

But Sir Toby's true feelings are revealed when they both appear, wounded by Sebastian, having mistaken him for the cowardly Cesario, in one of the cruellest exchanges in the play. Sir Toby is of course absolutely plastered:

SIR ANDREW I'll help you, Sir Toby, because we'll be dressed together.
SIR TOBY Will you help? An ass-head, and a coxcomb, and a knave, a thin-faced knave, a gull?
    (Act V, scene i)

And they both exit, helped by Feste and Fabian, to lick their physical and emotional wounds.

Sir Andrew has arrived in the household full of excitement, ready to woo his friend's niece, although there is no real feeling of emotional attachment on his part, or physical passion. He has taken the dancing, fencing and singing lessons, but all the self-help books and purchased skills in the world are no substitute for natural ability and stomach-churning passion. He is continually used for Sir Toby and Fabian's amusement, as another distraction from the grinding torpor in a house of mourning, and Sir Andrew is dizzily unaware of it all. He is, as far as he is concerned, surrounded by geniality and warm friendship and is having the time of his life, carousing and helping with Malvolio's gulling, with the promise of a new wife at the end of it all. How can his bid for Olivia fail with his friend Sir Toby's help? And at the end of it all, what does he leave with? An empty purse, a bleeding head wound and the terrible feeling not only of rejection by someone whom he felt to be an ally, but also the gradual realization that the only reason for his invitation was Sir Toby's sport.

By far the clearest, most lasting image of Sir Andrew that I have, however, is after the raucous hilarity of the carousing scene. It's the calm after the storm. Malvolio has severely chastised them all for singing drunkenly in the middle of the night and they have determined to have their revenge. There are glimpses of self-knowledge in Sir Andrew. His hair is lank; he knows he's not terribly witty, '. . . but I am a great eater of beef, and I believe that does harm to my wit'. His reasoning is rather suspect (though BSE *had* just taken hold during the run of our production, which provoked an uneasy laugh unforeseen by Shakespeare), or academic: 'I would I had bestowed that time in the tongues that I have in fencing, dancing, and bear-baiting. O, had I but followed the arts!' And out of the stillness of Act II, scene iii, in reply to Toby's comment about Maria, 'She's a beagle, true-bred, and one that adores me: what o' that?' he replies, 'I was adored once too.'

The simplicity and poignancy of that line in performance cannot be overestimated. And we will never know who it was that adored Sir Andrew. It could be mother, lover or sibling, even a loyal pet, but it suddenly brings this character whom the audience have laughed at into sharp focus. It's a line that suddenly gives him a past, a depth and a gravitas. He ceases to be a purely comic confection and becomes full of dark melancholy. In a play about love it's something that brings the audience up short. It's the distillation of lost love.

The bubble of pomposity

The first time Malvolio opens his mouth onstage he unwittingly adds to his eventual undoing. Feste, an outsider, living literally on his wits, has a long memory. Not only does Malvolio insult him in front of his employer as he is trying to win back his old position, but he questions his professional ability:

> I marvel your ladyship takes delight in such a barren rascal: I saw him put down the other day with an ordinary

fool, that has no more brain than a stone. Look you now, he's out of his guard already: unless you laugh and minister occasion to him, he is gagged.

(Act I, scene v)

It is the worst possible insult at the most sensitive moment. Feste throws these *exact* words back at him in the final scene of the play, invoking, like Viola, an unshakeable belief in Time:

But do you remember 'Madam, why laugh you at such a barren rascal, and you smile not, he's gagg'd'? And thus the whirligig of time brings in his revenges.

(Act V, scene i)

Feste has also been biding his time, nursing his hatred, knowing that in the just, karmic world he inhabits, the world of Illyria, order will be restored. Revenge is exacted on Malvolio and not only by Feste. He is an infuriating boss to work for, an exacting, humourless jobsworth with delusions of grandeur. He inspires loathing and the desire to prick the bubble of his pomposity in his employees and is, in Olivia's words, 'sick of self-love'. He has a rich fantasy life that becomes his Achilles heel, and the sharp-eyed Maria is the one to identify it. She knows that with very little prompting his arrogance will lead him to believe he is at the centre of Olivia's heart. He is isolated, friendless – one person's trusted family retainer is another person's exacting employer – and over time his devotion to Olivia has changed into a secretly boiling passion.

However, Olivia's giddiness is also not to be underestimated. As she falls for Viola in the guise of Cesario, she emerges from the chrysalis of mourning. Her behaviour changes and with it the atmosphere in the household, and this also helps to prompt Malvolio to further extremes. Is headiness catching? When

Olivia falls, she is surprised to find, 'Even so quickly may one catch the plague?' And in terms of structure, it's interesting to note that Olivia's gloves-off declaration of Act III, scene i –

> Cesario, by the roses of the spring,
> By maidhood, honour, truth, and everything,
> I love thee so, that maugre all thy pride,
> Nor wit nor reason can my passion hide.

– comes shortly before Act III, scene iv, where Malvolio is at his most open and reckless in his declarations.

The strength of his desire and social aspirations is such that the merest suggestion is enough for him to come leaping out of his severely ordered, stiflingly trussed-up existence in full, technicolour, yellow-stockinged glory. The pressure cooker explodes, and he not only humiliates himself completely and publicly, but has time to reflect and discover the full extent of his shame and humiliation. That he can even walk into the daylight and face Olivia after his incarceration is testament to an underlying inner steel; and as he has been so cruelly treated, who knows what will be exacted on his enemies after the end of the play? He has stripped himself emotionally naked, and hell hath no fury like a tightly wrapped Englishman scorned. I always find his curse at the end of the play chilling: 'I'll be reveng'd on the whole pack of you!'

He has been revealed to be a man of seething, overwhelming passions, all the stronger for being concealed. What started as a light-hearted prank has become something altogether darker. A man has been emotionally and professionally destroyed. The scenes in which he discovers the letter and then appears cross-gartered in yellow stockings provoke hysteria in the audience and give room for great front-cloth bravura from the actor playing Malvolio; but in retrospect, when he's locked up, it's been like gleefully watching a car crash. There's relief at not being involved and horror at the extent of the damage and the underlying feeling that, however ludicrously his pomposity and contrasting erotomania are portrayed, there but for the grace of God . . . Affairs of the heart are dangerous – we make ourselves vulnerable – and Malvolio is a glaring example of one of our deepest romantic fears made flesh: rejection. Even the most successful relationships suffer from an imbalance of ardour from time to time. And Malvolio – well, he couldn't be more deluded in that respect. He has shown his romantic hand in the full belief that he will be willingly accepted and, like a bicycle crashing into a Sherman tank, he is completely destroyed.

Structure

Look behind you!

I came fully to appreciate Shakespeare's *structural* skill, the simple placing of the scenes, only after months of playing in front of very varied audiences – from rowdy schools matinees that involved heckling and missile-throwing to reverential Friday nights, when the tickets were more expensive and people were determined to get their money's worth (not great laughers). Up until the end of the first act, the audience, like Viola, don't know Sebastian's fate. They have met all of the characters with the exception of Sebastian and Antonio (and Fabian, I know, but I've always been a bit bemused by him, a sort of shadowy Mr Fixit who appears when there is mischief afoot – bookie or gardener?). What turns the play from potential tragedy to comedy (albeit a dark one) is the placing of the first appearance of Sebastian. Straight after Viola's unsuccessful wooing of Olivia (unsuccessful in terms of lodging Orsino in her affections) Sebastian and Antonio appear. Sebastian is *not* dead. For the first time the audience is ahead of Viola. We are suddenly in the world of a Shakespearean comedy and, like the breaking of Olivia's vow of isolation, it is only a matter of when and how they will meet, not if. He is bound for the court of Count Orsino, where Viola now works. Coincidence? Or the subliminal psychic connection of the identical twin? I believe the latter. The parallels are already mounting up. They have both been rescued, believing their sibling to be dead; and both make for the household of the man mentioned by their late, beloved father.

Viola is then accosted by Malvolio (Oh God! not *him* again, she thinks), and she is left bemused when he leaves her with a ring that Olivia claims she left behind. The audience, meanwhile, have that slightly skittish 'Look behind you!' energy, having just met Sebastian. They are more immediately engaged, and it allows Viola to realize the ludicrous dilemma she is in, freed from the burden of mourning. The comedy can flourish, as the audience have been let off the hook by Sebastian's survival. The placing of the scenes helps the performer. I felt supported not only by Viola but also by Shakespeare. The play is a relay race for a great ensemble. It's no single character's play, and once the confusions and conflicts of the plot kick in, all the characters are swept along by it as it spins to its inevitable conclusion.

Viola is, by this point, on a high. She stops to consult the audience. As well as the immediate plot dilemmas she faces (the realization that Olivia loves her), she is beginning to fill with a sense of the true freedom she possesses. She is in a newfound land. As she is immersed further into the world of Illyria, she is always true to herself, but has the benefit of newness, in the same way as people can find themselves liberated by travelling abroad alone. In disguise she can paradoxically be more herself than ever before and discover new strengths. She is unstifled by the baggage of other people's knowledge of her previous existence. I know that, underlying this, she is bereft, but her post in Orsino's court gives her a purpose and a way of existing and living both with herself, and with the raw absence of Sebastian. Viola brought home to me the paradox that perhaps we can only truly be ourselves in the company of strangers. With a parent we will always be a child; to an old acquaintance we will remain largely the person they first met; and our actions and behaviour will be interpreted through that particular prism. As we change with each new experience that life throws at us, we are lucky if we are given room for that growth by our friends and loved ones. We can be stifled by people's fixed ideas of us.

This new-found freedom gives her confidence. She feels deeply for Olivia's predicament, seeing Olivia's love for her (Viola) in the same light as her own love for Orsino – as hopeless. But the situation is ludicrous, frustrating and, for the moment, insoluble. She can laugh at it; and she calls on her ally Time to help her: 'O time , thou must untangle this, not I, / It is too hard a knot for me t'untie.'

Shakespeare is now setting the plates spinning. Out of a beginning filled with bereavements and solemnity he has made two young women fall hopelessly in love, and brought an identical twin brother back to life, both sets of circumstances combining to promise maximum confusion later. The final plate to be set spinning is that of Malvolio's downfall. As I've said, Sebastian's emergence brings us to comedy. Viola can temporarily shrug off Olivia's romantic position. The carousing scene can take place in the middle of the night in order really to antagonize Malvolio, so that he can threaten to report them to Olivia, which is the straw that breaks the camel's back and drives Maria, Feste and Sir Toby to stitch him up with a success beyond their wildest dreams.

'Come away, death'

Orsino, meanwhile, is still demanding music, nursing his passion for Olivia. At the beginning of Act II, scene iv Viola is drunk with happiness, now totally at ease with her environment and revelling in the confidences and proximity of the man she has fallen for. They are in tune with each other. The music he has demanded strikes a chord with her. She immerses herself in it and when Orsino asks, 'How dost thou like this tune?', she replies, 'It gives a very echo to the seat / Where love is thron'd.' It touches her heart. Her abandonment to the moment immediately provokes Orsino to study her more closely. She has a wisdom and emotional maturity beyond her years to begin with, but when these are presented within the carapace of an even younger boy (Cesario), the effect brings Orsino up short. He realizes that this boy has experienced love, and quizzes him. Viola in effect tells him to his face that she is in love with him.

DUKE

What kind of woman is't?

VIOLA

      Of your complexion.

DUKE

She is not worth thee then. What years, i' faith?

VIOLA

About your years, my lord.

Her confidence and ease at this point in the play are a joy. She looks directly at Orsino, and her joviality can easily be interpreted by him as the embarrassment of confession, rather than as real amusement at the irony of the situation. The audience and Viola are in league with each other, both fully aware that she is truthfully addressing the object of her affection.

The conversation then takes a different turn. Orsino feels that Viola's supposedly female lover is too old for her:

      Let still the woman take
An elder than herself; so wears she to him,
So sways she level in her husband's heart:
For boy, however we do praise ourselves,
Our fancies are more giddy and unfirm,

> More longing, wavering, sooner lost and worn
>   Than women's are.

Younger wives are more flexible and adapt to suit their husbands, thereby ensuring their continued affection. Orsino is all too aware of quixotic male fallibility. Viola cannot help but agree. He goes on to state an unfortunate truth often borne out by experience:

> Then let thy love be younger than thyself,
>   Or thy affection cannot hold the bent:
> For women are as roses, whose fair flower
>   Being once display'd, doth fall that very hour.

For a man in love who believes himself to be in love with a distant, beautiful woman on a pedestal he has put his finger on the fundamental flaw in love based on external beauty: once a wife married for her beauty is past it, she will be traded in for a younger model; and from the light-hearted irony of the previous exchange Viola is suddenly confronted by darkness. She may be young, but she feels the march of her old ally, Time. She continues his simile, ostensibly lamenting the death of the rose immediately after it has attained its full, beauteous perfection; but the dark melancholy of *Twelfth Night* is at work here, and a young girl is forced to confront the transient nature of female physical beauty: '. . . alas, that they are so: / To die, even when they to perfection grow.'

Feste is found to sing the song that Orsino is anxious to hear. He is freelance, so to speak – is attached to Olivia's household but takes his wages and opportunities wherever he can; or, as he puts it: 'Foolery, sir, does walk about the orb like the sun, it shines everywhere.' And it is his song, the lyrics of which are completely unexpected by Viola, that suddenly brings back to her the loss of her brother, her only remaining family member. Listening to the song, she has a chance to be still, for leisure and reflection, something she has been avoiding ever since she made the decision to become her dead sibling. The effect is devastating for her. She is expecting a song that '. . . dallies with the innocence of love, / Like the old age.' This is what she actually gets:

> Come away, come away, death,
> And in sad cypress let me be laid.
> Fie away, fie away breath,
> I am slain by a fair cruel maid:
>> My shroud of white, stuck all with yew,
>>> O prepare it!
>> My part of death, no one so true
>>> Did share it.
>
> Not a flower, not a flower sweet,
> On my black coffin let there be strewn:
> Not a friend, not a friend greet
> My poor corpse, where my bones shall be thrown:
>> A thousand thousand sighs to save,
>>> Lay me, O, where
>> Sad true lover never find my grave,
>>> To weep there.

Sebastian is brought to the front of her mind. A song about wanting to die because of the rejection of a lover becomes something even blacker. The words resonate of a body lost at sea that will never be found or mourned over properly. In her mind's eye she sees him struggling to survive the storm, as she herself struggled. She sees him losing his fight for life as he is sucked down under the waves.

'Extraordinary how potent cheap music is,' as Noel Coward put it 300 years later. In the stillness, as she absorbs the delicately melancholy melody and lyrics, rational thought is hijacked and Viola's gut-wrenching grief surges up, threatening to overwhelm her. She struggles to contain it in such a public environment. However, the all-seeing outsider Feste clocks her and I believe sees through her masculine disguise, helped by her vulnerability. He also discerns and hints at Orsino's unacknowledged feelings for Viola. For all Orsino's protestations of love and constancy for Olivia, Feste says, 'Now the melancholy god protect thee, and the tailor make thy doublet of changeable taffeta, for thy mind is a very opal.'

It's the fool's luxury to speak the truth to the rich and powerful without fear of recrimination. Orsino is inconstant; his affections are changing without his knowledge.

A wonderfully blinkered misogynist

Suddenly, all except Viola are dismissed and she and the Duke are alone together onstage. Although they have been alone together before offstage (Orsino has already 'unclasp'd' to Viola 'the book even of [his] secret soul'), the audience are privy to their relationship at its most intimate for the first time. There is an air of expectation. The relationship has deepened through familiarity, and this time Viola has been knocked off-centre by her emotional turmoil and is less guarded. There is nothing like bereavement to inspire irritation with triviality or self-delusion. Having experienced at close quarters life's great certainty, death, and with the words of 'Come away death' ringing in her ears, Viola has little time for further encouraging Orsino in his romantic delusions. So when Orsino, having listened to his current number one love song, persists in instructing Viola to go yet again to woo Olivia, she confronts him with the reality of the situation, as Olivia's words, 'I cannot love him,' echo in her head: 'But if she cannot love you, sir?'

She tries to shake him into realizing the futility of his suit. He will not countenance failure with the simple statement, 'I cannot be so answer'd.' He is infuriating to Viola. She tries to put it in words of one syllable or to draw him the emotional equivalent of a simple diagram; and it becomes very personal. They have what I always saw as their first domestic argument. She illustrates the problem by presenting him with a picture of herself in clear, monosyllabic language:

> Say that some lady, as perhaps there is,
> Hath for your love as great a pang of heart
> As you have for Olivia: you cannot love her:
> You tell her so. Must she not then be answer'd?
>> (Act II, scene iv)

Ever the realist, she has already accepted that her feelings for Orsino are unlikely to be reciprocated. (She isn't to know that she's in a play, after all.) But he will still not face up to the truth. He launches into an attack on women, extolling the belief that they are incapable of true, deep-seated passions – a direct attack on Viola herself:

> There is no woman's sides
> Can bide the beating of so strong a passion
> As love doth give my heart; no woman's heart
> So big, to hold so much: they lack retention.
> Alas, their love may be call'd appetite,
> No motion of the liver, but the palate,
> That suffers surfeit, cloyment, and revolt;
> But mine is all as hungry as the sea,
> And can digest as much. Make no compare
> Between that love a woman can bear me
> And that I owe Olivia.

A wonderfully blinkered, misogynist and emotionally ignorant declaration, prompted by his fear of amorous failure.

Viola is provoked into such a naked declaration of her feelings that, even though she has more self-knowledge than all of the other characters in the play, she is forced really to confront the emotional stasis she is in; and her four-word response to his ludicrous outburst is so loaded: 'Ay, but I know—'

She knows firstly how unbearable unrequited passion is; she knows all too well that Orsino is wrong, wrong, wrong as she stares at him full in the face, a living, breathing example of a passionate, loyal woman. She knows too much for her years. She knows the wisdom and pain brought by bereavement. But above all she knows a lot more about emotional truth and robustness than Orsino; and then she tells him again that she loves him:

> My father had a daughter lov'd a man,
> As it might be perhaps, were I a woman,
> I should your lordship.

Although everyone in the theatre apart from Orsino knows the reality of the situation, she still maintains her disguise; but then, what would she gain from revealing her true identity? She would risk emotional rejection, of course. However, by this stage in her life as Cesario, having lived so successfully as a boy for so long, on call as a member of the household twenty-four hours a day, Viola must seem a lifetime away for her – indeed, a painful memory for her, as Viola is a girl who has lost her brother, but Cesario is a valuable member of Orsino's household, a charming, efficient boy who is the image of her beloved Sebastian. Viola has, in effect, died; and it is not until Orsino (intrigued by the first mention of family from Viola/Cesario and of this extraordi-

narily passionate woman) asks directly about her, that with a
jolt Viola has to remember the history of who she really is.

> A blank, my lord: she never told her love,
> But let concealment, like a worm i' th' bud
> Feed on her damask cheek: She pin'd in thought,
> And with a green and yellow melancholy,
> She sat like Patience on a monument,
> Smiling at grief.

She presents her current state as a history and looks to the
future for the first time. It looms large and empty for her. She
sees herself clearly, past, present and future all in an instant.
She will have her youth drained from her by time and her concealed passion. Her bloom will disappear, subsumed by grief
for her brother, and she will never confront her loss but live in
limbo, waiting patiently for her life to end. Her decision to
conceal herself as a temporary measure to buy time and heal
herself suddenly has no end for her. She has no escape. Still
and serene, with no rancour or self-pity, she will continue to
be in close proximity to the one person (apart from her dead
brother) who will cause her most pleasure and pain: Orsino.

Then she comes back to life again. She has opened
Pandora's box for herself but struggles to slam the lid back on.
She becomes active. Her very existence proves Orsino wrong
in his assumptions about the fairer sex. He favours declaration, noise and operatic turmoil as proof of passion and constancy; but Viola's description of this still, silent figure, waiting
and constant without even a declaration of feeling, an invisible acolyte, shocks him. He sees there is another, even truer
path. 'Was not this love indeed?' Viola asks; and as Orsino tars
all of womankind with the same brush, so Viola, having
proved her point, does the same for men:

We men may say more, swear more, but indeed
Our shows are more than will; for still we prove
Much in our vows, but little in our love.

Viola feels that often masculine protestations of love are simply that – protestations – with no real feeling underneath. Or
men are simply more suggestible, and as they can talk themselves into love, so they can achieve the reverse. I agree with
her. But then I would, wouldn't I? Orsino's innocent inquiry,
'But died thy sister of her love, my boy?' (death being the
ultimate proof of feeling and constancy) opens up another
yawning chasm beneath her feet. 'I am all the daughters of
my father's house, / And all the brothers too; and yet, I know
not . . .'

She is the only daughter; she has described herself in vivid
detail. Then, because of her outward physical appearance, she
is forced, again, to put into words exactly what she has been
avoiding by taking refuge in Orsino's household. She is her
only brother. But even that isn't certain. She doesn't know his
fate for sure and – as has been described so often by people
waiting for news of loved ones, perhaps in a war zone or terrible disaster – the not-knowing is almost harder to live with
than the certainty of death. Life stops. One is pulled exhaust-
ingly between hope and grief. The words 'and yet I know not'
are almost impossible for Viola to utter.

Then her extraordinary inner steel snaps back, and an even
more urgent need for displacement activity: 'Sir, shall I to this
lady?' She has had her most public display of grief since being
shipwrecked on that empty Illyrian beach. There has been a
little relief. She has finally admitted her true situation to herself and to the man she loves. But she finds most comfort in
activity and professionalism. She has been still for too long
and has been surprised by her grief, so she makes Orsino send

her spinning out again, to press his hopeless suit. Only this time he has armed her with a gift. But then he has still to learn that it takes more than jewels to get a girl to fancy you.

This scene is crucial to the final resolution between Viola and Orsino. A conversation ostensibly about the strength of male versus female love is something much more poignant for Viola. Although Orsino is not aware of the true resonance of Viola's words, a new interest is pricked in him. He learns from Viola the error of his outburst, even if it's simply a dawning realization that he is not always right. More importantly, he looks at Viola/Cesario in a completely new light. She suddenly has a past, a family, even, and knowledge of life gleaned from experience – unusual in one so young. It's as if he sees her for the first time as she is, suddenly in the spotlight. By the end of the scene he is inextricably bound to her.

Kisses

I do want to add a footnote to the above examination of Act II, scene iv. The production was punctuated by kisses. Olivia kissed Viola at the height of her infatuation. Sebastian kissed Antonio, thanking him for saving his life and for his invaluable help in Illyria, both financial and practical. Antonio kissed Viola with great sadness when he believed her to be a treacherous Sebastian. Matinees full of schoolchildren were always a trial. Uneasy with any demonstration of affection at the best of times, and no doubt encouraged by each other to be as disruptive as possible, they were extremely vocal in their reactions. No one had warned them that there would be kissing in the first place, let alone girls kissing girls and boys kissing boys on the mouth. By the time the actor playing Antonio moved in to kiss Viola in Act III, scene iv there were anticipatory groans of disgust when he'd only got within six feet of me. However, the first of these kisses was between Orsino and Viola, and it came just before the line, 'Sir, shall I to this lady?' It was equally passionate on both sides, an important contrast to the others in the play. Orsino is moved by Viola's description of this patient yet passionate girl, and by her distress at the unknown fate of her sibling. It is a spontaneous act on both their parts, completely in the moment – an act of comfort on his side that turns to sexual attraction, and on her side the unexpected realization of a dream. But it marks an irreversible turning point in their relationship. It has deepened and strengthened, and whether a production has a kiss or not, the emotional exposure in the scene, which is simply in the text, achieves the same end. As I've said, Pandora's box has been opened. And I like the way that it is Viola, not Orsino, who brings matters back to some semblance of normality by suggesting another trip to Olivia.

Whether it's because of a directorial kiss received from the man she loves, or simply from the memory of emotional intimacy, Viola now has a spring in her step. She knows how to do one thing exceptionally well: serve her master. And that is what she determines to do. Her life is by no means a bad one – the long dark watches of the night from the previous scene are over for her – and like the Pandora myth, although her situation has changed irreversibly, hope is left cowering in the shadows as a consolation. She has reminded herself that although she feels Sebastian to be lost, she doesn't know the exact truth and, buoyed up by Orsino's empathy, she may allow herself to think that he may still be alive. But all this is soon forgotten as she begins to be sucked further into the plot.

She sets off for Olivia. She meets Feste, the all-seeing, all-knowing fool. They are alone. He has seen her at Orsino's and his curiosity about her, like that of most of the other inhabitants of the play, has been awoken. Who is he? Or is it *she*?

Viola is witty, challenging Feste and paying him for his jesting, but she will not let him 'pass' upon her. Feste like Viola is a great watcher. He may be earning some cash from her, but he also has the opportunity to satisfy his curiosity about her and scrutinize her up close. She is all too aware of this and enjoys his wordplay, but will not willingly let herself be the centre of attention, not because she cannot hold her own, but because she knows that, of all people, he is the most likely to see through her disguise. And indeed he has. He hints at it: 'who you are and what you would are out of my welkin.' The fact that, of all the possible ways of thanking her for her money, he picks 'Now Jove, in his next commodity of hair, send thee a beard!' is very telling. Outwardly of course it is a sentiment wishing a speedy puberty on a callow youth, which prompts Viola's reply: 'By my troth, I'll tell thee, I am almost sick for one [i.e. Orsino], (*aside*) though I would not have it grow upon my chin.' But this sudden tiny discourse on gender is too close for comfort for her and so, again, she tries to continue with her mission with, 'Is thy lady within?' Feste has eyes like a hawk, he misses nothing. If he has glimpsed Viola's true identity, an alliance of outsiders is formed. There is no risk of betrayal and a mutual respect forms between them. He is a good fool, and she is not only bright and witty but has managed to convince all she meets that she is a boy – no mean feat. It is also a much richer option to play right from their first meeting in Orsino's house, and they both need as many friends as they can get.

Alarm bells ringing

Viola has to put up with Sir Toby again and also meets Sir Andrew for the first time. Immediately she unwittingly sows the seeds for the duel that is to come. He greets her in French and she replies effortlessly, which throws Sir Andrew slightly. Sir Toby indulges in some rather laboured wordplay, which Viola ridicules, and then Olivia mercifully appears, putting a stop to it. Olivia, though initially silent, is *thrilled* to see Viola, and this is not lost on Sir Andrew, whose sole purpose for visiting is to win Olivia for himself. How does this youth do it? What's his secret, his infallible technique for getting the girls? Sir Andrew stops and takes mental notes and is witness to Olivia, unable to contain herself, requesting of Viola/Cesario, 'Give me your hand, sir.' The alarm bells start ringing and he leaves, crestfallen and ripe for Toby to plant the idea of a duel in his head.

The alarm bells also start ringing for Viola. All right, she had an idea that Olivia had fallen for her, but she has no idea that she has actually gone bonkers. Olivia has got it bad. It all seemed so simple to Viola on the way over: just stick to the job in hand, ignore or deflect any mention of Olivia's feelings for her and simply press Orsino's suit. But life is never that simple. As Viola is anxious to keep things formal, so Olivia is determined to ignore Orsino's embassy and find out as much as she can about this marvellous youth. There is a polite tussle between them, until Olivia tires and blurts out,

> O, by your leave, I pray you!
> I bade you never speak again of him;
> But would you undertake another suit,
> I had rather hear you to solicit that,
> Than music from the spheres.
>
> (Act III, scene i)

Oh dear, she wants a declaration from Viola/Cesario. Viola is cornered. All she can say is: 'Dear lady–', before she is interrupted. She is in a ludicrous dilemma. She has enough grace and humanity to want to let Olivia down gently. But how can she even begin to steer the conversation into safer waters?

47

She is also tormented by her feelings for Orsino and has great sympathy for Olivia, as their respective situations are identical in terms of unrequited love. She could so easily have lost control with Orsino in their last encounter and blurted out *everything*, completely humiliating herself in the process, and she has a growing feeling that Olivia is coming close to doing just that. If Viola/Cesario doesn't declare his love for her, Olivia is so giddy, having just stripped off the heavy carapace of mourning, that she may just go too far.

Olivia confesses to sending the ring after her, laying herself open to hurt – an act of faith. She has shown her hand and simply says, 'so, let me hear you speak.'

'I pity you,' is all that Viola can say, but of course Olivia is entirely unaware of just how pregnant with meaning that simple phrase is. Olivia desperately seizes on that as a sign of affection, and Viola finally has to be cruel and to the point: 'No, not a grize: for 'tis a vulgar proof / That very oft we pity enemies.' Love has nothing to do with pity, girl, and if you only knew what rivals in love we really are.

Viola and Olivia are effectively enemies at this point. Olivia relents and Viola's relief is almost tangible. She thinks Olivia is not going to declare her feelings fully. She is formally dismissed – thank God! – and, ever hopeful, Viola asks, in spite of Olivia's previous pronouncements on the subject, if there is any message at all that she wishes to send Orsino. 'Stay,' says Olivia, and finally perhaps Viola's steadfastness in the face of denial has paid off – perhaps Orsino will get a second chance. Viola turns back, full of expectation, she's got what she came for at last. But *no*. All Olivia asks is, 'I prithee tell me what thou think'st of me.'

Oh bugger, think quickly, quickly. Viola has been completely wrong-footed, and there is a wonderfully sinuous exchange between them. Olivia asks what Viola thinks of her:

VIOLA

That you do think you are not what you are.

OLIVIA

If I think so, I think the same of you.

VIOLA

Then think you right; I am not what I am. [Too right!]

OLIVIA

I would you were as I would have you be.

VIOLA

Would it be better, madam, than I am?
I wish it might, for now I am your fool.

Viola feels trapped, ridiculous, and extremely fed up as she snaps this last line back at Olivia. And of course, rather than being put off by this, Olivia is entranced. Turning to the audience, almost swooning she mouths to them, 'O, what a deal of scorn looks beautiful / In the contempt and anger of his lip!', the Shakespearean equivalent of 'My God, he's beautiful when he's angry.' And not only is she not rebuffed, it is now or never, she is spurred on to make her declaration, and having been bottled up and bound up by formality for so long, it comes pouring out of her in rhyming couplets. It's as much as Viola can do not to try to hide from this relentless barrage of words:

Cesario, by the roses of the spring,
By maidhood, honour, truth, and everything,
I love thee so, that maugre all thy pride,
Nor wit nor reason can my passion hide.
Do not extort thy reasons from this clause,
For that I woo, thou therefore hast no cause;
But rather reason thus with reason fetter:
Love sought is good, but given unsought is better.

Viola feels as if she's drowning in a vat of treacle. She must extricate herself. She tells the truth:

> By innocence I swear, and by my youth,
> I have one heart, one bosom , and one truth,
> And that no woman has, nor never none
> Shall mistress be of it, save I alone.
> And so adieu, good madam; never more
> Will I my master's tears to you deplore.

She vows never to return. But of course she does, when Olivia, desperate to see Viola/Cesario, tempts her back with the possibility that she may still be persuaded to love Orsino – fat chance – and Viola escapes, breathless and confused.

Sir Andrew is encouraged by Sir Toby and Fabian to challenge his rival for Olivia – Viola – to a duel. He writes a letter, which is such rubbish that Toby discards it and decides to set them on to each other by telling each of them that the other is a borderline psychopath and a highly skilled swordsman. He must be *so* bored. Meanwhile Malvolio, having found the anonymous letter lying in the garden, has been tricked into running round the house, smiling and wearing yellow, cross-gartered stockings. And Sebastian and Antonio make a second appearance. They are nearing Orsino's court but decide to separate and meet later at the Elephant (an inn). Antonio lends Sebastian his purse, just in case he sees anything he would like to buy.

So Viola goes back to Olivia a third time, hoping that she can finally be persuaded to love Orsino. But it's hopeless. Olivia's final words to her were just a ruse to ensure the object of her desire returned. Olivia has a certain dogged quality to her devotion, rather like Orsino. She is very hard to shake off and she is in danger of entering a rather dreamlike fantasy land. Despite Viola's numerous rebuttals, she is found at the beginning of Act III, scene iv planning her welcome for Viola/Cesario: 'I have sent after him, he says he'll come: / How shall I feast him? What bestow of him?'

Olivia is unshakeable in her devotion. No matter what Viola says to her, she will not take no for an answer. She is possessed by the madness of love, and the situation is more insoluble because she has a complete awareness of the strength and potential danger of her feelings. As she says to Viola, 'A fiend like thee might bear my soul to hell.'

Viola stops to try to catch her breath, clutching a jewelled picture of Olivia that has just been pressed into her hand. What's a girl to do? Suddenly Sir Toby and Fabian appear, bringing desperate news that terrifies her. A knight is waiting for her at the orchard end, baying for blood. Whatever she has done to offend him, he wants a fight, to the death. And as Fabian says, 'He is indeed, sir, the most skilful, bloody, and fatal opposite that you could possibly have found in any part of Illyria.' Not good news then. But of course the 'fatal opposite' is Sir Andrew. She has no recollection of any offence and comes close to revealing her true identity. What a way to go – in a duel, pretending to be a boy, having survived a shipwreck in boiling seas. Sir Toby is not one to miss out on any sport whatsoever, and there is no escape for her.

When they are finally facing each other, each terrified by their opponent, it's hard to tell who is the bigger girl. Viola is reluctant to draw and Sir Andrew is quaking in his lovely tights. I don't think Viola is particularly unskilled at fencing, brought up in a household full of men: her brother and father. I have strong images of them as children, fighting each other with gusto, as most siblings do, and I'm sure Viola has an armoury of Chinese burns, punches and enviable fencing skills. However, the biggest weapon in the arsenal is fear, and Sir Toby knows this only too well. They are pushed to the brink of a brawl, when suddenly, a miracle. A tall, skilled swordsman appears and stops the fight, taking Viola's side:

> If this young gentleman
> Have done offence, I take the fault on me:
> If you offend him, I for him defy you.

And no sooner has he appeared than he is taken into custody, arrested at the suit of Count Orsino. Who the hell is he? Of course, the audience know him as Antonio and they immediately sit forward, waiting for the delicious spectacle of mistaken identity.

This stranger advances towards Viola. He is happy to be arrested for her sake, but he needs some money to help himself with in custody. He asks for the return of his purse. Viola is literally speechless. Who *is* he? She stands silent, frantically checking her memory for the slightest clue as to this solicitous stranger's identity, but there is none. Receiving an unabashed declaration of love and gifts from the woman that the man you love is in love with, then being challenged to a duel by a maniac for no apparent reason, and then being asked for the return of a purse by a complete stranger who saves you from death by stabbing would certainly try the most patient of people. Viola, however, has spent the whole of the play improvising and adapting to unusual surroundings; it's just another day in Illyria for her, and she goes with the evidence she has – it's all she's got. She does not know this man, who seems to be becoming distressed at her lack of recognition. She offers him money out of gratitude for saving her. This enrages him. He has asked for the return of his purse and speaks of previous generosity to her on his part. She simply does not know him and tells him so, and is equally ignorant of former kindnesses to her. He is dragged away by his captors but is moved to speak by Viola's apparent betrayal of him. He tells of saving her life and of his subsequent devotion to her; he is desperately hurt by her lack of recognition of him. Then suddenly he addresses her by name. However it is not her own but that of Sebastian, her dead brother. The name roots her to the spot. She cannot speak and can only watch as the saddened stranger is led away. The full import of his words begins to sink in. Her deepest, most sacred desire has been brought to the front of her consciousness. She has been distracted by activity, infatuation on the part of herself and others and by mischief on Sir Toby's side. But now she has real, tangible hope after all these months in emotional hiding, and she confesses to the audience the real reason for her disguise as mentioned previously: she has become her brother. She leaves to return to Orsino. It's been a full day for her.

Unravelling

As Viola fell for Orsino almost instantly, Sebastian behaves in a very similar way with Olivia. He is met in the street by a fool who insists he knows him, but manages to pay him to go away. Then he is set upon by a drunkard and a lanky, long-haired knight, who assault him for no reason, and he has no option but to draw his sword. The fight is prevented by a woman. But what a vision she is. In the midst of his confusion she appears, dismissing his assailants with stern authority, then turning to him with eyes full of devotion and apology. She invites him to enter her house and says that she has lost her heart to him. Is he dreaming? A successful conquest without the awkwardness of wooing or declarations? If he is dreaming, he prays he doesn't wake up; and if he isn't, well how could he let such a wonderful opportunity go? He looks at her and, taking her by the hand, he jumps off the emotional cliff with her. He is smitten. With the three words, 'Madam, I will,' his life is now hers.

The next time we see them together she brings a priest in tow with the words, 'Blame not this haste of mine,' and asks for his hand in marriage. She knows her own mind and, having won the heart of her Cesario, she is not going to rest until they are permanently linked by matrimony. Sebastian simply says, 'I'll follow this good man, and go with you, / And having sworn truth, ever will be true.' The simplicity and truth of the feelings and statements on both sides, clear-sighted and unflurried, make us believe that this match is made in heaven (even if Olivia is not marrying the boy she fell in love with).

Orsino finally emerges from his lair to visit Olivia in person for the first time in the play, with Viola in attendance. She is on edge. She cannot forget the encounter with Antonio and, more importantly, if Olivia is still as devoted to her, how will Orsino react? Not terribly well, one suspects. She can only cling to formality, her duty as an invisible servant and the faintest hope that Olivia has calmed down. Viola has told him of the duel with Sir Andrew and her rescue by a stranger (but not, one feels, of her encounters with Olivia) and then, as they are waiting for Olivia to emerge, Antonio appears. Viola may not recognize him, but Orsino certainly does. They are old enemies. Why would a wanted man make himself vulnerable to arrest in the street? Antonio reiterates his story of devotion to the youth standing by his side – Viola/Cesario – and his betrayal by him. Viola is mesmerized. Antonio is the link to her brother, but again they are overtaken by events and Olivia appears. Viola tries to make herself inconspicuous, but to no avail. She had hoped that Olivia would conceal their supposed intimacy, but she seems more proprietorial than ever. Orsino is volatile. He is in public for the first time in the play, not within the safe confines of his household, and this makes him vulnerable. He seems to emerge blinking into the sunlight. All the months of devotion to Olivia have robbed him of the gift of being casual and, to add to his febrile air of paranoia, Olivia seems more interested in his servant. She even silences Orsino publicly. He shifts from nought to unreasonable in the space of five lines and is prompted into the most remarkable declaration of love for Viola. He has paid homage to Olivia for months; he has built a shrine in his heart to her and cannot believe that she will not have him. What does he have to do to win her? Olivia, of course, simply tells him to remember himself, as his mood becomes black and unreasonable. He can see what has been happening under his nose. The messenger has usurped him in her affections. He is apoplectic and his thoughts turn murderous. If he can't have Olivia, perhaps he should kill her so that no one else can?

> But hear me this:
> Since you to non-regardance cast my faith,
> And that I partly know the instrument
> That screws me from my true place in your favour,
> Live you the marble-breasted tyrant still.
> But this your minion, whom I know you love,
> And whom, by heaven, I swear I tender dearly,
> Him will I tear out of that cruel eye
> Where he sits crowned in his master's spite.
> Come, boy, with me; my thoughts are ripe in mischief:
> I'll sacrifice the lamb that I do love,
> To spite a raven's heart within a dove.
>
> (Act V, scene i)

The momentum of that speech is unstoppable. Viola is transfixed, consumed by her feelings for Orsino, and these words are out of her mouth before she has time to think: 'And I most jocund, apt, and willingly, / To do you rest, a thousand deaths would die.'

We are suddenly in a different, darker play. Viola will do anything for him, especially after his unintentional declaration. However, the mischief of the plot kicks in; and the rhythm of the verse helps to turn this potentially grisly scene into one of comedic confusion, especially if played at speed. Orsino and Viola are exchanging heartfelt rhyming couplets, but Olivia is now secretly married to Sebastian, whom she believes to be Cesario. So when confronted with the spectacle of her new husband proclaiming devotion unto death to Orsino she is distraught, especially as Viola/Cesario's choice of words is rather unfortunate:

OLIVIA

Where goes Cesario?

VIOLA

      After him I love

More than I love these eyes, more than my life,

More, by all mores, than e'er I shall love wife.

Orsino is trying to remove Viola; Olivia wants her to stay, believing her to be her husband. She calls the priest to confirm her secret marriage. This is startling news to Orsino and even more so to Viola. All these revelations emerge publicly in jagged, rhyming verse, with Viola in the centre shocked, confused and spinning.

OLIVIA

Ay me detested! How am I beguil'd!

VIOLA

Who does beguile you? Who does do you wrong?

OLIVIA

Hast thou forgot thyself? Is it so long?

Call forth the holy father!

DUKE

      Come, away!

OLIVIA

Whither, my lord? Cesario, husband, stay!

DUKE

Husband?

OLIVIA

      Ay, husband. Can he that deny?

DUKE

Her husband, sirrah?

VIOLA

      No, my lord, not I.

Again she doesn't have time to think about her brother; she can cope only from moment to moment. And at this moment she is baffled. Then Viola's hopes are raised. The priest appears. She knows she hasn't married anybody. She will be let off the hook. But it's not her day: the priest confirms Olivia's story. She now has to face Orsino's wrath. But he does something even more terrifying to her than the torrent she expects. He is shocked at the depths of his servant's supposed betrayal: so much duplicity in one so young. He looks Viola coldly in the eye, tells her to take Olivia and never to come near him again.

The plot is reaching maximum confusion, as is Viola, who at this moment is near despair. She has been accused of duplicity and betrayal on a monstrous scale – all this against a girl with a strong moral centre. To add injury to insult, Sir Andrew appears with a bleeding head wound and, of course, accuses Viola of injuring him. Finally, Sir Toby comes limping in, drunk and bleeding, and cruelly tells Sir Andrew what he really thinks of him: 'Will you help? An ass-head, and a coxcomb and a knave, a thin-faced knave, a gull?'

Olivia is heartbroken: her new husband has forgotten their nuptials. Orsino no longer has a devoted servant, Viola, or an object of devotion, Olivia. Antonio has been denied twice by the boy he rescued and is languishing in custody, and Viola has lost the trust of Orsino, her reason for existing. Something has to give.

My father had a mole

She is standing bereft. She cannot see a way forward. The recent events have been so dreamlike and intoxicating she even questions her level of consciousness. Viola hears Sebastian's voice first. She comes to, turns and stares and stares. Sebastian. The bereaved's dream can be a comfort, but imagine if it really were to happen – how would we react? Viola is in a state of shock, disbelief and fear. She cannot speak, her heart is thumping against her ribs. She sees her brother and hears him, but is he an apparition, a figment of her imagination? Sebastian sees a mirror image of himself. He has never had a brother. Who is standing before him? He questions her. Viola is trying to see through a fog, shocked by the dead walking and terrified that he might disappear again for ever. In her terror, Sebastian can see through the masculine exterior and his sister is gradually revealed to him. He asks this figure before him formal questions: '. . . what kin are you to me? / What countryman? What name? What parentage?'

Her replies confirm her true identity: 'Of Messaline: Sebastian was my father; / Such a Sebastian was my brother too.' Then she points to Sebastian:

So went he suited to his watery tomb.
If spirits can assume both form and suit,
You come to fright us.

She is petrified of this vision before her, desperate to believe that it is what she has wished for from the beginning of the play. She has named Sebastian and he becomes flesh.

Then Sebastian looks at Viola in her terror:

> Were you a woman, as the rest goes even,
> I should my tears let fall upon your cheek,
> And say, 'Thrice welcome, drowned Viola.'

He calls her by name – the first person to do so since the shipwreck – and so she is called back into existence, not only for him but for herself as well. Their tentative joy grows with the realization that they are both living, breathing flesh. Their language becomes beautifully simple:

VIOLA
> My father had a mole upon his brow.

SEBASTIAN
> And so had mine.

VIOLA
> And died that day when Viola from her birth
> Had number'd thirteen years.

Such a specific physical reference for their father gives an immediate warm glimpse of a close-knit family. Perhaps it was something that, as small children, they were fascinated by, or the butt of affectionate family humour, rather than just a simple distinguishing mark. Then she recalls the death of their beloved father, the last traumatic event to befall them both before the shipwreck. Even after confirming that they are indeed brother and sister restored to each other, Viola still cannot bear to be embraced by – or indeed to embrace – her brother. It is all still too new and she is not fully restored as Viola. She is still in her masculine disguise. She can completely become Viola again only when her brother is there to witness her restoration, and when she is sure beyond a shadow of a doubt that he will not be lost a second time:

> If nothing lets to make us happy both
> But this my masculine usurp'd attire,
> Do not embrace me, till each circumstance
> Of place, time, fortune, do cohere and jump
> That I am Viola . . .

Finally, having been brought back to life after his utterance of her name, she utters her name herself. It is a moment of wonder for her after months of concealment; she has not so much supressed her own identity as succeeded in actually becoming Cesario, a masculine version of herself, with all the new-found freedoms that that has entailed. She has come to take that life for granted – *that* has become the familiar – and she must now strive to become herself again with the aid of her brother. The potency of names and identity is vividly illustrated here. Sebastian and Viola name each other. They breathe each other back into existence. They are two halves of the same being, identical twins, and can fully exist only with each other. They are at peace and have finally reached dry land.

The twins then realize they have an extremely bemused audience. Orsino especially is unsure whether or not to be tentatively ecstatic. His mind is churning, looking back on his relationship with his young male servant, who has just revealed himself to be female. I think that the key to Olivia and Orsino accepting and wholeheartedly embracing the truth of their respective situations lies in the conviction with which the twins' reconciliation is played, not just by the twins themselves but by every single character on stage. What they have just witnessed is far from commonplace. Even before Sebastian has uttered the words: 'Do I stand there? I never had a brother . . .' the amazement of the onlookers is voiced by

Olivia when she says, 'Most wonderful!' She cannot believe her eyes. There are two marvellous boys standing before her. It is not the world of clunky Victorian melodrama and its attendant sentimental coincidences. It is a time for the restoration of the natural order, both spiritual and physical, for the end of a need for emotional healing. Mourning and confusion are over and life can continue, with all its pitfalls and misfortunes, but with renewed vigour.

The time it takes for the twins to realize fully who they both are, gives the onlookers time to reassess their deeply felt emotions to the person they knew as either Sebastian or Cesario. In the face of the terror, relief and joy that Viola and Sebastian go through in an extremely short time, any niggling doubts evaporate in Olivia's and Orsino's minds. Order is restored with the twins' reconciliation. Olivia may have fallen in love with one twin and married another, but the time she has spent with Sebastian is enough to convince her of the blissfulness of her situation. Orsino, unsurprisingly, takes slightly longer to clarify the situation for himself. He has to make the biggest imaginative leap. Boy has to become woman for him. He cannot see Viola as female immediately: 'Boy, thou hast said to me a thousand times / Thou never should'st love woman like to me.'

Viola, with Sebastian found, has no fear left, and leads Orsino gently towards the truth:

> And all those sayings will I over-swear,
> And all those swearings keep as true in soul
> As doth that orbed continent the fire
> That severs day from night.

There is no doubt in her heart. The scale of her simile is as all-encompassing as the 'willow cabin' speech she made to Olivia with Orsino in mind. He meets her halfway, taking her by the hand, but asking to see her in women's clothing. He can't quite make the leap yet. Then there comes the most lumpen piece of dialogue I had to deal with. After scenes of passionate declaration, magical rebirth of the dead, comes this:

> The captain that did bring me first on shore
> Hath my maid's garments; he, upon some action,
> Is now in durance, at Malvolio's suit,
> A gentleman and follower of my lady's.

Of course it is logical that the Captain has her female clothing. But then for him to have met and been imprisoned by Malvolio, 'upon some action'? It's rather vague, *does* reek of Victorian coincidence, is never fully explained and is a rather clumsy device to swing the narrative back to Malvolio. Shakespeare needed a way to lead up to Malvolio's final appearance, or perhaps he simply had a tight deadline; but I did wonder about that offstage story. The Captain and Malvolio – what happened? and was Malvolio wearing his yellow stockings at the time?

The resolution of Viola and Orsino's story is halted temporarily. In the midst of joy, the darkness of *Twelfth Night* comes through. Viola has not been privy to any of Malvolio's downfall. Indeed, her last experience of him was of a pompous, patronizing jobsworth who didn't bother to conceal the contempt in which he held everyone, apart from himself and his mistress Olivia. It is chilling for her to hear how far he has fallen. A prank has spiralled out of control, driven by spite. Not content with humiliating Malvolio publicly by utilizing his own arrogance, Feste, Sir Toby, Fabian and Maria have caused him to be incarcerated as a lunatic. Feste, Viola's erstwhile ally, brings on a letter from Malvolio that is literally a cry in the dark, written in the dankness of his prison cell, asking for justice. Olivia sees at once that his words are not the incoherent ravings of a madman and orders him to be brought to her. Fabian leaves to fetch him.

Finally free of torment

While they wait for Malvolio's arrival, it is Olivia who finally prompts Orsino to clarify his feelings for Viola. He still hasn't asked for her hand in marriage. As I have said, right at the beginning of Viola's journey, in order for the emotional triangle to be resolved, a fourth person needs to appear and someone in the circle has to turn round and notice what they have taken for granted all along. Sebastian has appeared, captured Olivia, and now Orsino is gradually realizing the true meaning of deeply felt affection, love and respect, rooted in an unexpected source: his pageboy Cesario. He no longer has to fight surprising feelings for his servant. I mean surprising in the sense that Orsino considers himself to be heterosexual. But the whole notion of 'inappropriate' feelings is a modern imposition on an Elizabethan text. Men have loved men and women have loved women since time immemorial. Orsino has fallen in love with a boy – with his mind, his spirit. Gender has become irrelevant. He is in possession of a curious creature. I don't think it's too much of a stretch to say that the play ultimately allows anybody the possibility of falling in love with the person they are meant to, regardless of gender. The uniqueness of each individual is what will ultimately form the lasting bond of a couple, regardless of sexual attraction, which may fade over the years – though, to contradict myself completely, I always had a sneaking suspicion that the sex was absolutely fantastic between Viola and Orsino when they eventually got round to it. They have no secrets any more. But then I am a ludicrous romantic.

My lord, so please you, these things further thought on,
To think me as well a sister, as a wife,
One day shall crown th' alliance on't, so please you,
Here at my house, and at my proper cost.

These are the words from Olivia that finally prompt a formal proposal from Orsino. She even offers to pay for the joint nuptials that she proposes. If you can't marry me, at least be my brother-in-law. This is the licence that, subconsciously, Orsino has been waiting for to complete the shift he has to make in order to see Viola completely and clearly as his true partner:

Your master quits you; and for your service done him,
So much against the mettle of your sex,
So far beneath your soft and tender breeding,
And since you call'd me master for so long,
Here is my hand; you shall from this time be
Your master's mistress.

He accepts her as an equal and submits himself to the dangers of true emotional attachment. He jumps off the cliff with her, like Butch and Sundance. He is finally free of torment.

At a point in the play where everything seems resolved, and people expect Viola to rush offstage to reappear in a lovely big girl's dress for a fantastic double wedding, the spectre appears at the feast: Malvolio. What a pitiful figure he presents in contrast to Viola's previous memory of him. A man of precision, conscious of immaculate presentation and correctness at all times, has been reduced to a shivering wreck. He has been kept in dark, solitary confinement save for the teasing of Sir Toby and Feste. He has been punished out of all proportion to his misdemeanours and although, as Miss Prism says in *The Importance of Being Earnest*, 'The good ended happily, and the bad unhappily. That is what fiction means,' his reduction to his present state is undeserved. He was only guilty of the sin of Pride. But it is Feste who reminds him of the beginning of his downfall: his criticism of Feste's professional skills, proving the old adage that comedy is a serious business. His wrongdoing is exposed, with unknown consequences for his tormentors, and he leaves the stage like the bad fairy at the christening, screaming the words, 'I'll be reveng'd on the whole pack of you!' The play ends in a wonderfully minor key. The four lovers leave to face their future together, happy for the moment, but facing the pitfalls that life and time will inevitably throw at them; and so Viola's journey is complete.

The thing is, when you're performing a play, it's work in progress. Things are in a permanent state of flux. There are, of course, certain basic truths in the performance that remain pretty constant, but if you're striving for the perfect performance (which you will never achieve – or if you think you have, change professions), you have to be open, questioning. You must try new things every performance, intentionally or unintentionally. Even within the most rigidly blocked performance by the most dictatorial director, there is room for experimentation. Why bother? Well, the aim is to keep alive – to keep the characters and the world of the play living – and to let the audience in. In the twenty-first century when, realistically, the theatre is competing with all of the other media and is simply just another alternative to DVD, cinema and television, now more than ever each opportunity is precious. Live, communal experiences are magical. These plays are not museum pieces; they are continually performed because they are living, breathing accounts of humanity with all its flaws and merits. The poetry helps to take us out of the everyday, appeals to us emotionally, bypassing our heads and hitting us straight in the stomach.

As in Spanish Golden Age drama and the works of the great Russian dramatists, tragedy and comedy go hand in hand in Shakespearean comedy, and scenes can change from one to the other in a line. If all that dark melancholy is in place, as in *Twelfth Night*, how much levity is earned. Great comedy comes out of pain, and for Viola her dark sadness means that she has a forward energy – not perkiness, like some deranged child star, but an openness to experience, a wide-faced acceptance and wisdom. In terms of playing her, no matter what was happening in the outside world – no matter how tired or distracted I was – without fail that immediately disappeared when I stepped out on to the stage. We could all learn a lot from her.

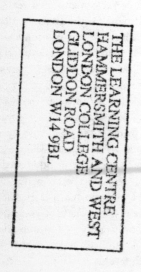